MIND *FRAGMENTS*
DE L'ESPRIT

MIND *FRAGMENTS* DE L'ESPRIT

ALLISON AUBE-MARTIN

atmosphere press

NOTE FROM THE AUTHOR:

"Everything around you is material for you to see and stretch out. Seek out the essence and make it your own."

My starting point for this poetry book came in the midst of a pandemic for which isolation from people and passions was at its peak. Picture a night owl, writing and writing, with its only source of light the brightness of a screen, while the city is dead, reaching for the only movements and intrigue one can get access to when silence is the new background noise: the thoughts of the brain. Not those of a conversation in a restaurant where ideas are being projected and overlapped on the fly, not those you have to forcefully extract when speaking up in class, but these other ones floating high above, being ignored—that is, until the right time comes and the highest ladder helps you taste them. Think of the world I'm offering you as one of a spider's web. Every beginning, middle, end, shift of direction, lines joining at a corner; they all have a role to play in the unity of the structure; might they seem to have been created in a messy and disconnected way at first. Most precisely, think of the world as a brain, as the mind. I perceive the latter as a whole enigma that needs to be cut into little pieces for us to better understand the layers and levels. Some writers think about form and structure and find themselves to find the key to their whole story around a magnificent bright mechanic. As for me, I connect to the idea, the message, the memory, or the experience I want to get across that is screaming inside and happen to find the words along the way, experimenting with significance and tone, intention, and rhythm. I express to share the meaning and then discover the architectural aspect of the text, a beautiful play of rhymes and repetitions.

Mind *Fragments* de l'Esprit is a universe that approaches two realities of the same perspective. Identity in expression of viewpoint but also identity in language.

If you happen to be afraid of words because they have broken down your expectations in the past, see that I am not making any promises, but rather simply offering elements of an exchange. Art is discussion, denunciation, guidance, clearance. Art implies an invitation for action as a collective. I invite you all to read them aloud and let the stories impact you. Je vous encourage à les lire à voix haute et à les laisser vous toucher. "The pages are afraid you'll turn them too fast."

Special mentions in the photographs:

Wishing I could be that girl: Elisa Schu
Discovering what lies under these traits: Annie Tai
Nonchalant drop on the floor: Yolaine Fleury
Medea: Amanda Gao

To you, my readers

I have no doubt you will take good care of my words

Let's all begin now

BLINDING SIGHT

The spotlight
Hit me
Too bright toward my face
I swear I couldn't see
I am all alone, expected
To move
To breathe
To scream
I know the lines, but I am focused on the steam
This airy
Smokiness
This heavy
Atmosphere
From impulse, I perceive my darkest fear
Am I dreaming or are you really here?
Your condescending smile, your cocky smirk, your penetrating gaze
I thought god would come,
am I amazed
Amazed the devil would care to come again
Care to wait
Wait for me to grab the bait
Time is ticking, my body is shaking, the audience is sighing
This fifth time, may it be
the last time
Everything's frozen, yet winter has not arrived
I see you threatening me, but don't you remember
I survived
My wounds have healed, the marks
you left have sealed
I focus
on the crowd
I dream
of my voice being this loud
As heavy and rich as a thundercloud
I fill my lungs as wide as possible and dare
Dare to begin, dare to win
Oh, what have I missed?
Has the devil already hissed?
The steam is gone
My fear is gradually passing out
Looking back, the creature is on its way
And I'm standing onstage waiting to blow them away

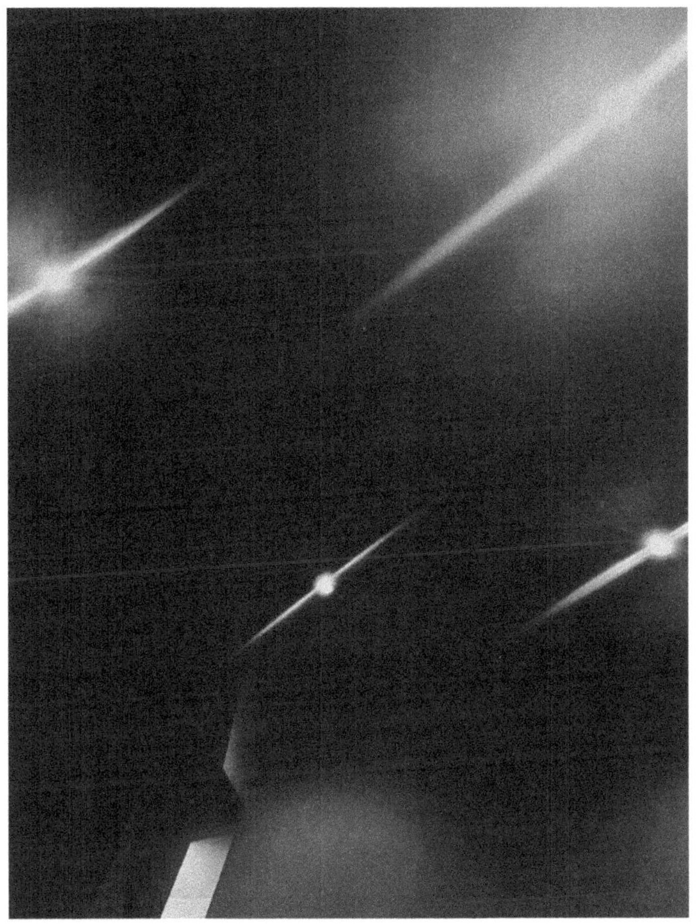

FEELING THE BLUES

Feeling the kiss of the sun against my damp skin
Is my heaven
Poisoned of venom
I see a miserable bird trapped in a metal cage
Looking back
Looking ahead, with the use of a knife
I set the bird free
Sobbing apologies
I perceive my reflection in a million mirrors
Right below
On my left, bubbles are floating around in the air
On my right, I'm sitting in a cold forest in the middle of the night, not
    being needed elsewhere
On my diagonal is standing a royal queen of fierce and cold authority.
Then pitch-black soul. Humidity. Dampness. Coldness.
I disgusted myself by not making others a priority
Eyes opening, I realize
All these pieces were only fiction
Of my goofy yet pure imagination; they were stories
I was only feeling the jazzy blues of a Saturday night
Not realizing the world kept turning and my eyes receiving
Flickers of a red light

WISHING I COULD BE THAT GIRL

I am a simple girl
In my jeans and sweatshirts, I catch and hurl
I don't glow from afar; I have no interest in putting on a show
Don't even get me started on relationships, I gave them up a long time
　　ago
I keep my hair long and knotted up in masses
I keep my hazel eyes hidden behind some glasses
One glance from across the room, and you'd assume I get As in all my
　　classes
I rarely smile
People must think I'm hostile
When in reality, I'm just trying to go unnoticed, to keep a low-profile
Oh god, when entering this world, I must have chosen the wrong file
Now, I'm just pacing around comparing and wishing
Wishing I could be that girl
In her floral dress, I could twirl
If only she knew how much she radiates
I bet she gets plenty spur-of-the-moment dates
Her short silky hair, her green almond-shaped eyes
One glance from across the room and you'd surely get hypnotized
I wish I could have her smile
This curve of the road, traveling a thousand kilometers a mile
This sensual couch that could manipulate an entire crowd during trial
Her words are well-calculated, mannered and soft-spoken
Why is it my words leach out of my mouth so crude and broken?
My mom tells me I think too much
But I am confident my brain is my personal touch
I may not smell of flowers freshly cut
I may want to remain silent and shut the world out
But inside my head, everything's thought out
In this cocoon, I lack any insecurity or doubt
As for today, my thoughts and vision are not shared
But for the right time, be ready, I'll come prepared
Prepared to show what is circling, what is agitating, what is spinning
I wish to have her confidence, I wish to move an entire audience
Time is of the essence—soon enough, I'll need to procure evidence.
Evidence of my worth
Evidence of my dominance

SWIMMING THROUGH MY FEARS

I am a swimmer, always have been
In this discipline, I chose loneliness and convenience to win
In no need of trainers or friends, I did it all to tell my story
I worked hard for a muscular and lean body
I transformed my suffocated breath into a controlled one
I paid for quality swimsuits so I couldn't be overrun
I rehearsed the technicality of my craft
Nothing to hold me back at last
Nothing to take away the medal
Everything was under control; I had a strong mental
Then, one day, as I rode toward the nearest beach
As I entered the immensity of water
As I slowly started to smile underwater
I got trapped
My natural habitat suddenly turned against me, knife in the back
Meteorology promised a calm and serene ocean
A blue tranquility, a stillness, a creamy lotion
But what I got was a rocky dark; life hanging on by a thread
Waves crushing over my head
My breath submerged with agitated thoughts
The numbness of my body, the heaviness of the moss
My lungs coughing salty water
I was freezing to death
In this instant, I confess
I needed help,
The cards were dealt
I needed to be saved
Hope faded

Then, it appeared out of nowhere
A large boat, unaware of my scare
Full of people, full of laughter, full of joy
I looked over them in admiration
This terrible weather really didn't seem to affect their vibration
I was struggling all along while they were having the time of their life,
    away from the tension
It was as if the sun had come back, the wind had slowed, and the
    ocean had calmed
A hand stretched out over me, an invitation for me to grasp,
At first, I was hesitant, not knowing if I should accept or gasp
But I acted on impulse, let down my barriers, and got on board.
In coming to my senses, I realized I would be dead if they had bailed
I was so sure of every little detail

I never anticipated the unpredictable, the game of the lord
God, was I oblivious!
Thinking that for so long, I could do it on my own
Stuck on my own island, following my own terms
May the wind take away my pain
May I swim through the fear
May I never be alone again

LETTING GO OF RESISTANCE

You thought you
Could easily disappear
At every turn you
Refused to hear
Already planning in your mind, you had your fate aligned
Persuading yourself of your inutility
And believing in this fatality
You stepped outside
And
Jumped in the hole
Letting go, you gave gravity control
Control
Over your body, over your destiny
You were really near the end
About to crash
Like an airplane
But instead, I saw you land
Your graceful figure reduced to bones
The air filled with painful groans
You calculated
Everything
Down to the core of wanting to stop
Feeling
And I still find it confusing
Why risk breathing if it's to live suffocating?
Washing down infliction with severe addiction
Why leave loved ones behind?
Finding yourself damaged and confined
You've spent your whole life trying to
Quickly fix
When all you needed to do was
slowly
put back
together
the bricks

SEX AND US

For me
Why is it represented by the act of giving a flower?
For you
Why is it represented by the act of winning a war?
If I get touched, my purity has been damaged and killed
If you get touched, your masculinity has taken power and strength
He gets to come home a champion
I get to return home ashamed and dirty
He gets to feel pleasure without pain
I simultaneously experience both
He gets to buy flowers without paying any taxes
I get to buy only one for the price of four
I scream no at the top of my lungs, yet I'm unheard, muted, ignored
He screams no at the top of his lungs, yet a pause is taken, time stands
    forever still
For a woman to refuse an intercourse, she must be confused, surely,
    she is ignoring her true impulse
For a man to refuse an intercourse, he must have gone mad, surely, he
    is going out of his mind
For me it's crude and raw physical violence
For you it's giggles and being mocked heavily and repeatedly
I fake an orgasm and I'm a bitch
He fakes an orgasm, it's a matter of a simple glitch
Society has differentiated both sexes, according to Mars and Venus
According to one Penis and one Uterus
And yet, both Adam and Eve were naked before eating the forbidden
    fruit
It is not the woman's fault men are easily manipulated in dispute
It is not the man's fault women are tempted by the possibility of deep
    knowledge
Both wanted a way out of this oppression absolute
Sex is only a matter of shallow distinction, don't you acknowledge?
Reactions differ, but deep down, everybody is driven by the same things
To be free and to deploy our wings

FEAR IS ON THE STREETS

Too confident and
I'll attract
Too weak and
I'll get trapped
On the subway, I focus on the floor
On my way home, I carefully lock the door
I am mocked when wearing a baggy outfit
When really
I'm afraid of getting hit
How does a skirt or dress become an Invitation?
Have you not seen
my agitated walk?
Have you not seen
the earplugs in my ears?
Have you not seen
my internal cry for help? No, you haven't
Stupidly clueless about any crucial signals
You walk, seek, observe, choose, approach in the hope
Of hearing some giggles
Whether you were polite, whether you blocked my route
What gives you the right?
The right to compliment my butt area
I should be grateful you said? Oh well thank you I forgot I simply had
    hysteria
In these intimidating moments, reaction is well observed
Acting polite and I suddenly led the guy on
But hey, I show some teeth and suddenly
I'm the brutal Oregon?
One lie left to spit
The teenager bit
I am only seventeen
I say innocently
And suddenly
The man gets bit by chivalry
What will happen when my thirties I'll reach
Words can say so much
But getting old is a common touch.
One last look from behind my hood
Thank god, he is gone for good

ONE DAY, YOU WILL

One day, you will stop counting down calories
One day, you will stop envying these galleries
One day, you will start smiling in the mirror
One day, you will start looking at the paintings a little clearer
For now, you look at the scale, not liking the number
For now, you're ashamed of your work, putting on a cover
You want a perfect feminine body
You want to be as good as Dalí
Every day, you skip meals
Every day, you peel away your drawings, as they seem too unreal
In this overachieving pattern, you have stopped enjoying
Going to the restaurant and ordering have you boiling
Going to an art show have you comparing
If you close your eyes, can you appreciate the taste of cake
If you close your eyes, can you follow your hand, trusting in the process
    without taking a break
Enough with the labels, enough of the numbers making you feel ashamed
Enough with society's hierarchy making you feel drained
One day, another girl will want to look like you
One day, another girl will want to paint like you
The grass always looks greener on the other side
But I promise you, if you close your eyes and let go of your pride
You'll start seeking what you need
And stop believing in achieving what makes you succeed

DESTRUCTIVE LOVE

I was entirely consumed by your being
Every time I looked at you, I felt as though I was falling
Little did I know this temporary state could get me killed
Driven by naiveté and innocence, with shame and guilt my heart was
    filled
You attached the harness
I was all buckled up and ready to taste the sweetness
The sweetness of love
Love, this word that no one dared explicitly embark upon
That would come just like another one is gone
My friends warned me about pleasure, playfulness, and tenderness
But I entered another gate
I had keys for another destination
Obsession, possession, manipulation, reclusion
I landed on a concrete floor
Others get to fall on this cloudy mattress
I opened the door
To find you lying down with this mistress
Without words, how could you have let me be this witness
You made your choice, you let me leave for good in stillness
It's crazy how you played me over
And over and I kept forgiving
Trying to reach the shore
To effortfully keep swimming
I had to avoid drowning, avoid losing you and the pain
That came along
But I now know I have to see what it's like with you
Gone
I am standing on a high-fence wire, fierce and strong
Watching the love birds passionately get along
Captured I'll be again and feel like I belong
Entering a scene and distancing myself from the monologue
But captivity is not a necessity
I have to focus on me
I have to search the key in this black sea
Yes, you may have
Left
Yes, you may have suffocated me with
Pain
But truth be told, I have
Remained

INVISIBLE ME, VISIBLE YOU

Made out of delicate glass and rough wood
It is how I'm understood
Made out of emptiness and profound pain
Here's how I consistently maintain
Composed with
A rigid trunk
No one could depict if
I ever get drunk
Only perceiving the outer of thee
I can only see you, thus I have never seen me be
I know every little scar that lies on your skin
I know this specific birthmark that shall never leave your chin
You are clearly visible
To every pair of eyes
I am invisible
Always in disguise
One day, I am reflecting the master I so adore
The next
I am projecting an image of terrorizing traits one should never have bore
I can make you feel the prettiest or ugliest person in the room
You'd either throw this satisfying grin or shed a tear in a tiring exhume
And while
Some other objects might find this responsibility of major capital in
    society
I must shout
I've had enough of this never-ending anxiety
Everyone forgot about variety, now it's only a matter of notoriety
When are we going to cease focusing on material goods and property?
I look around and I wonder
Why of all
did I have to be a mirror?
Shoes got the adventurous spirit; for them, the sky's the limit
Pens got the brain
Never in restraint
They write masterpieces of books
Transmission of a melody that instantly hooks
Pianos got the subtility of the touch
And I got the outside matière, the superficial subjectivity worthy of a
    myth

For now, my owner agrees with the image she's faced with
But I deeply fear the day
The day one wrinkle will make it through the surface
And stand in the way
Oh no, did she think her rosy cheeks would last forever?
Well, I guess the trashcan is coming
Be weary of any brutal endeavor

CE N'EST QUE DE L'EAU

Ce n'est que de l'eau
Ce n'est qu'une gorgée du ruisseau
Tout n'est que quantité
Il ne faut simplement point perdre son identité
La soirée n'est qu'éphémère
Je veux bien que les sensations s'accélèrent
Des gestes mal placés, tout n'est qu'affection maladroitement partagée
Des baisers volés
La soirée ne fait que commencer
Un centième verre, je flotte dans l'univers
Verre mille, tout est à découvert
Tout est brouillard, tout me conduit au trou noir
Jetée dans les bras de l'ignorance
On me dirige vers une certaine itinérance
Aveugle et sourde
Je n'ai d'autre choix que de me perdre dans la foule
Danser
Me coller
Tomber
Me rattraper
Oublier
Au milieu de la tornade
Milieu de la rigolade
De la forte luminosité des portables
Je me sens vulnérable
Tous les organes de mon corps m'empêchent de signaler ces gestes
    intolérables
Je perds le fil, j'ai la tête qui vacille
J'aimerais bien retourner en ville
Tout allait bien au début, mais à la fin je pense hélas que j'ai trop bu
Ce n'est que de l'eau et pourtant elle me colle bien à la peau
J'empeste affreusement, un coup sur l'épiderme
Ma gorge me brûle terriblement, je me retrouve sur mon lit bien ferme
Hier n'est que souvenirs flous, je l'admets j'étais bien saoul
Demain promis je vais cesser Demain promis
Je laisserai le ruisseau couler
Mais pour l'instant il me faut dormir, il me faut récupérer
Dans mes rêves, il me faut me distancer de tout ce que j'ai bien pu réaliser
Je ne veux rien savoir, ne souhaite rien revoir

Mes amis ne cessent de m'appeler
Je refuse de goûter au mercure
Loin dans mes couvertures
Le mercure de la vérité
Le mercure de mes erreurs passées

EFFRACTION DE L'INSOMNIE

Je suis allongée
Je ne dors pas vraiment
Par effraction, l'insomnie est arrivée
Toute douce, me surveillant
Moi, je ne suis pas capable
Invisible, je ne la vois pas
Elle est plus forte que moi
Pas seulement cette fois
Mais bien pour la millième fois
J'essaye de la vaincre
Je pense à faire toutes les positions
Celles que j'ai vues à la télévision
Gendarme, étoile de mer
Rondin, fœtale
Il y en a trop
Je suis trop paresseux
J'en essaye seulement deux
Deux dont je ne connais pas le nom
D'une, sur le ventre
Fuck, j'ai trop mangé
De deux, sur le dos
Fuck, faut que j'aille voir un ostéo
Je ne fais pas de sport
Je ne vais jamais dehors
Dehors il fait sombre
Aucune ombre
Je n'aime pas la clarté
Peut-être bien que chus un vampire
Mais je ne bois pas de sang
Je n'aime pas le sang
Je mangerais plutôt des crêpes pour survivre
J'aime les crêpes

Bon-là j'ai faim
Allez, ne pense à rien
Fuck, elle est toujours là
Fuck, elle est tout le temps là
Faudrait que je pense à grand-maman
Grand-maman me parlant de politique
Mais on s'en calisse de la politique
De toute façon, on va tous crever bientôt
Bon-là, je m'énerve trop
Inspiration, expiration

Expiration, inspiration
Je compte les moutons
Un, ça ne fait rien
Vingt-trois, le noir est roi
Cinquante, j'ai là une insomnie fuyante
Soixante et un, je m'éteins
Quatre-vingts, Fuck elle sera sûrement là demain

27

DERRIÈRE LES RIDEAUX DE NEIGE

Je n'y arriverai pas, je n'y arriverai pas je crois
Mon souffle est court le long de mon coeur
Je porte une tonne de maquillage
Je me sens comme sur la plage
Comme un coquillage
Mon extérieur est dur et froid mais au fond, je suis molle
Comme les montres, comme la terre, comme l'œil
L'œil qui juge, l'œil qui se trompe, l'œil aveugle
À rester là à attendre, je suis enfermée comme dans un rectangle
Un enclos à moutons, trop nombreux, trop sauvages
Je me sens seule, au milieu des nuages
Ma tête se remplit de rires, de chuchotements, de bruits
Du silence
Tout se bouscule, bouge, démonte la réalité
Je pense
Ouvre les yeux Julie et cesse de rêver
L'heure approche et toi seule, tu le sais
Regarde les projecteurs danser
Regarde le volcan qui habite leur lumière
Oublie hier
Danse pour oublier la lune, oublier l'anneau
L'anneau qui tient Saturne en place
Tu vois la salle qui se remplit comme un aquarium
Les requins et les thons, même quelques poissons clowns
Tu les vois tous nager pendant que l'eau continue à couler
Et les heures défiler
Vivant est l'aquarium mais
Un homard est mort
Tu l'as tué par tes mots, par ton souffle, par ton corps
Tu fumes, fumer tue
Tu aimes, l'amour tue
Peter est venu à nu
Non pas Peter Pan
Non pas Peter Parker
Oui Peter Roy
Il est venu combler le seul siège qui comptait vraiment pour toi
Tu l'as vu pleurer hier
Il applaudira peut-être aujourd'hui
Il restera yeux levés, pupille claire
Cette nuit
Peut-être que le feu peut oublier l'eau qui l'a éteint
Peut-être qu'un photographe peut pardonner à sa muse
Je ne sais pas, je ne peux plus y penser

Je ne sais rien
Le roi du silence est arrivé
Il est temps pour moi de voler entre les lignes sur le lac des cygnes
Il neige sur scène, il
Neige dans mon costume, il neige
Dans mes pieds
L'hiver sera long, il ne fait que commencer

29

WITNESSING THE DEADLY LIVING

I saw her last May with her darling boy
Feet on the ground
I remembered her energy
Her strength and joy
Steven Doyle had her in his arms
One quick move
On went the alarms
Time went by too fast,
The ambulance belonged already in the past
Facts are she died in the snow
Facts are she couldn't be saved three days ago.
If only time could have been on my side
If only fear wouldn't have forced me to hide
Knife pulling out of a pocket, as sharp as the mind
Monster circling around, getting behind
I saw reluctance and disgust gaining in his expression
Could it be, he acted for such horror obligation
Could it be, the fruit of a misinterpretation
No, my head is set, murder only speaks for
Murder
Motive is only excuse
Only sneaky ways to conceal the bruise
I saw this clear and concise cut
I saw heavy dark blood dripping
Nobody warned me of the monstrosity of watching a killing
Not only one of a stranger, but this of a beloved
I pushed the emergency button in panic
Oh boy did I already know it was far too late
Already I saw coming this massive gate
A corpse shaking on the ground, tears violently shedding on my lips
The man must have heard my sadness to this madness
For he quickly gave an end
As last a memory could be
I went through this entrance away from violence
Away from this internal need for vengeance
Angels spreading their wings over me
The beloved joining me in harmony
Below on earth is chaos around death
Right there is celebration around releasing gulps of breath

PIÉGÉE DANS LE MONDE MANICHÉEN

Seule dans le salon, je m'envole
Étant chavirée autant par les dièses
Que par les bémols
Je me sens comme décollée du sol
Le toucher du blanc me fait virevolter, le noir au toucher
Me fait voyager
Si seulement le monde pouvait y ressembler
Dehors, tout est chaos et impulsion
Pourtant mon piano n'est qu'ordre et déduction
Je préfère sympathiser avec les notes
Tout est sûr et serein
Je ne tomberai jamais sur un assassin, ni d'ailleurs
Dans un ravin
La tête dans mes partitions
Je me suis persuadée de la beauté de mon univers
Ailleurs, jamais
Je ne trouverai un endroit plus sécuritaire
Mais, il m'arrive encore de regarder par la fenêtre
D'envier secrètement
Oh, oui les fillettes aux jupettes riant entre leurs dents doucement
Oh, oui les beaux garçons rétorquant des mots taquins
Tous ces faits et gestes ne sont que latin, ne sont que mandarin
Tout parait si fantaisiste, complexe et franchement
Hors de ma portée
Rien qu'à les observer, j'en ai déjà la nausée
Pourquoi jouer avec le feu
quand on peut ne l'avoir jamais déclenché
Pourquoi donner de l'attention au do
quand c'est sol qu'il faut jouer
Pourquoi garder cacher les mots
qui ne cessent de nous tourmenter
La fille a beau rigoler, je sais qu'elle ne l'aime point
Le garçon a beau la critiquer, je sais qu'il l'aime au plus haut point
Le monde est cruel rempli de sous
texte et
d'intentions entre
croisés
Quand pourrais-je enfin sortir et découvrir les choses comme elles sont
  présentées

J'attends encore
Que les mélodies soient ajustées à la bonne mesure
J'attends encore que les nuances se déplacent
Pour faire place à l'absolu
C'est seulement à ce moment que je pourrais me dévoiler
À nu

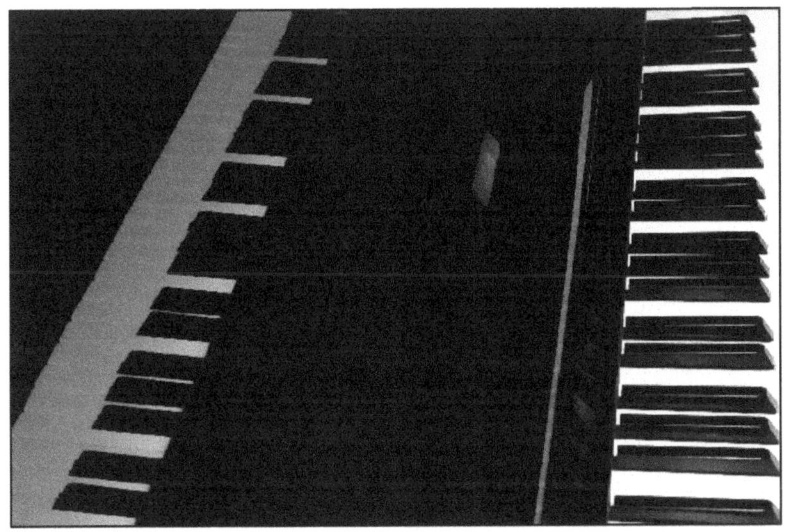

REMARQUER AUTRUI

Les autres voient que je mange pour me
Satisfaire
Au fond, je me prive pour
Plaire
Les autres voient mon sourire, pensant que tout est
Gagné
Au fond, mon âme est lourde et, par le temps,
Bien usée
Les autres remarquent mes ongles déchiquetés, dégoûtés de cette négligence
Au fond, j'ai tant essayé mais apparemment, rien d'autre n'arrive à
    combler cette absence
Les autres observent avec jugement l'interminable
Liste de mes relations courtes
Au fond, c'est avec elles que j'ai appris l'écoute
Du moment, du doute
Les autres ne comprennent point mon choix de carrière
« Elle doit sûrement être bête! »
Au fond, écrire et jouer sont passions entières
Aucunement la preuve d'une attirance pour les soirées coquettes
Les autres remarquent mon manque d'initiation à prendre les souvenirs
En parade
Au fond, j'aime voir la vie défiler plutôt que d'en garder une impression
Stoïque et froide
Les autres considèrent mes cernes
Recommandant le sommeil comme outil de suppression
Au fond, je reste éveillée toutes les nuits pour étouffer la pression
Les autres voient un corps athlétique pensant tout de suite à la génétique
Au fond, je me tue à avaler les séances de conditionnement physique
Je remarque sans cesse les autres
Rien n'est comme l'on suppose
Alors cessons de chercher la cause, de vouloir se tourner vers des remèdes
Des doses
Parler et commenter n'est que voie facile
Opinion n'est qu'arrogance et comportement versatile
Écouter amène à défricher les mauvaises herbes
Sur la route
Chut ; J'oublie les verbes
À part celui de : Écoute

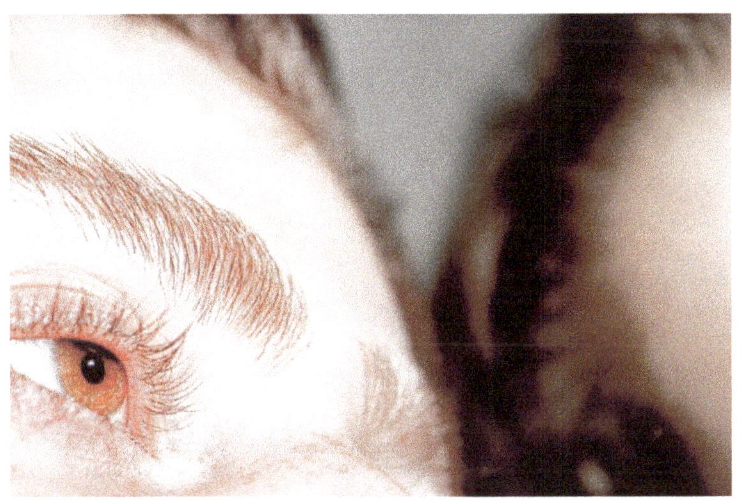

ENNEMI COMMUN DES MORTELS

À peine est-il arrivé
Dans nos vies
Nous commencions déjà à penser qu'il partirait
Tout en courtoisie
Jamais nous n'aurions pensé le sentir nous envahir
Sans pouvoir le percevoir, jamais nous n'aurions pensé qu'il puisse atteindre
Le monde comme la peste noire
Au début,
Les restrictions nous paraissaient bien méritées
Enfin une pause nette
Loin du capitalisme et du travail acharné
Mais assez vite
La réalité des conséquences et des répercussions a repris le dessus
Aux nouvelles
Le nombre de morts et d'hospitalisations a été reconnu
Des familles en pleurs, des populations en panique
Cet ennemi est dit cibler nos aînés et les personnes asthmatiques
Et pourtant, la peur était
générale, mondiale, monumentale
Munis de masques, de gants
De gels désinfectants,
Nous étions prêts à nous en débarrasser très rapidement
Loin de la vie active
Confinés dans des espaces qui ne vivent
Plus, nous avions déjà hâte de pouvoir revenir à une société
Moins perdue
Plongés dans l'espoir, nous continuons à lutter encore aujourd'hui
Contre tous ces dommages
Créés à cause d'une simple chauve-souris
Qui rôde dans les rues et quartiers toujours aussi vaillante et
Robuste
Injuste
Nous avons oublié que cette créature nous est commune
Brume
Dans la solitude et la crainte de l'autre
Nous nous sommes plongés
Nous nous sommes déterminés à ne rien attraper
Et pourtant quand nos masques seront enlevés et les distanciations
    rapprochées
Que restera-t-il de l'humanité
De notre sens de la collectivité et de la communauté ?

DOOMED TO BE WORKING THROUGH THE DOTS

I thought I had it under control, that everything would turn out okay
Sadly, I've gone way
over my head, thinking this feeling could fade away
You look at water; at first, you perceive it
as innocuous and serene
And yet, if you distort it
into ice in your imagination, only are you thinking you might quarantine
In a matter of seconds
everything is turned upside-down.
One second
You're laughing
And the next
You're experiencing a heavy meltdown
That's exactly how it felt being
In this cold labyrinth with
No way out, I was waiting for these three dots to lead me on
Lead me toward a complete sentence, the coming to a solution
I got trapped in this revolution
In the middle of the crowd, you'd be wearing your mask,
In vain, you'd want me to keep away from the secrecy that lays in that
    flask
I really tried but at the end of it, how can I shine in the darkness of your
    shadow
How can an optimist not be drained by the somber ideologies that you
    hold as a Scorpio?
I truly wanted to be with you under the bright rays of
The sunny sun
However, you only accepted to be buried in the snow, right next to
Your gun
If only I could have made you see the beautiful things that the world
    has to offer
Looking at a full glass, gliding through the clarity of water
But at last you will never change and neither will I
On the other side of the phone, you let your voice fly real high
Filled with determination, you were decisive and ready to talk
On my part, I kept nervously counting the seconds on my clock
I knew what would arrive
I was simply not ready to take the dive
Five words echoed in the room, five painful words.
There went an absolute ten seconds of *silencio* sneaking its way in some
    records

"I don't love you anymore I declare"
You simply declared
Maybe one day, the dots will take their proper place
But for now, I'm being haunted days and nights in a particular embrace
I envision you tasting the chase of the grace,
Be it, quit hurling yourself at any horse-race
But only in my dreams, I keep on believing
Reality hits hard, I will have to keep on forgetting

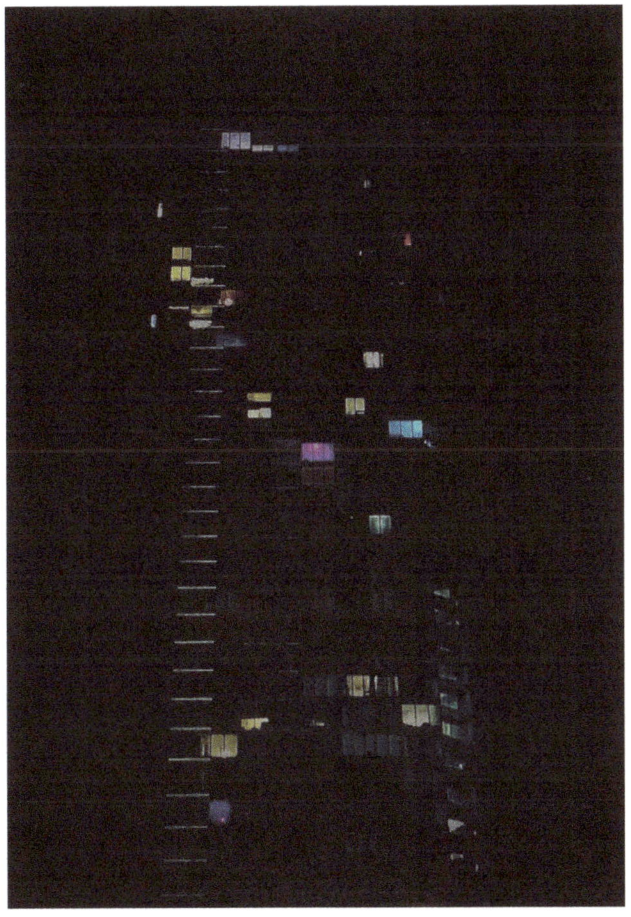

INTERNAL MONOLOGUE

You've been there since day one
You could have chosen anyone
In fact, you keep harassing
Everyone
Well I need you to leave
I've had enough of this thief
The happiest moments stolen
The darkest moments frozen
You keep on running
You keep on tracking every little thing
I need you to let me go
Or
I'll for sure let you win in a ring
I was born yesterday,
How come two steps forward
I cannot summarize
All of the sunrises, the cries
The flies and the surprises
All fallen from a cliff, of uncertainty there is a cave
I flee

Why won't you let me see?
I don't know which map I should follow
I don't know which pills I should swallow
Am I sure to not get trapped?
Do I have to seek a possible attack?
I may be guided
I am sure to be blinded
But I can't return, I know what awaits and
I can't advance, or I'll fall right into space

TRACE D'UNE DÉCISION FATALE

Une cicatrice en surface invisible à l'œil nu
Une histoire qui me paraît encore irrésolue
La jeunesse maladroite, des gestes bien impulsifs
Le sang qui coulait à flot devait être fort répulsif
Une fillette qui voulait seulement se faire remarquer
Perdue dans ses rêves, elle s'est vite faite remorquer
Un garçon fougueux qui courait trop vite
Hélas, il n'était doté d'aucun repère géographique
Une collision, une fraction de seconde
Le bruit se fait entendre, les corps retombent
La division est nette, les deux partis se font languir
Les observateurs ne savent quel camp choisir
Un ange est venu calmer le jeu
Les enfants ont cessé d'être nerveux
Les ailes ont parlé commettant l'irréparable sacrifice
Même si la faute appartenait aux deux pacifistes
Le consensus s'est fait sentir, c'est le garçon qui doit subir
Un mort suivi d'un blessé
La fausse justice a encore percé
Des secours portés à l'élu
Vingt points de suture ont été prévus
Le corps masculin a dépéri sous la terre
Moi qui pensais que nous avions progressé depuis Voltaire
La pensée s'est fait abattre par le revolver
La faute est humaine, on nous dit
Mais en vérité, c'est le hasard qui décide du sort des érudits

A CAUSE HEARD IN THE INACTIVITY

We pretend to care for their existence
But only
When it is made from a certain distance
We scream and shout for this cause on the street
But at home
We got no shame when it is time to eat
Slogans well-written intertwined with compassionate dialogues
Going to the market and selecting the right product, coming right from
    a catalog
Falling onto the floor
By the sight of these little paws
But out on the west, the leash is gone and so are the laws
Recording a video for YouTube
The necessity to be sensitized
I didn't realize you suddenly had become so wise
I saw you wearing your fur
The food chain exists nonetheless, why make it a social
Mess, fess, stress
We judge the plates of our neighbors
To yet forget to point our knives at the capitalist behavior
Why the need to brag for our moral conscious
Let it be from either beasts or leaves
Your kitchen is public, your recipes out in the open for critiques to be
    received
Treatment toward animals needs to be fixed
It is a given
But political expression
And oppression
Have again blinded us, hypocrisy has risen
Words count for nothing
Just articulation through a phone booth
Only actions care and dare speak the truth
No need to be ashamed of eating meat
No need to follow this vegan influencer just to tweet
Injustice is cruel from afar
Masking this issue as a trend can make you a star
No need to smile for the camera
I know how much it can create stamina

SORTIR DE L'OMBRE DE MON EXISTENCE

Cette boîte rouge posée
Sur mon chevet
Les bras tendus
Il me semble que j'en ai vu
Le reflet
J'attendais de sentir cette matière lisse et vernie
Je suis en retard, elle aurait déjà emprunté un chemin d'accès interdit
J'attends sur l'unique banc fraichement peint
Je succombe au grand froid jusqu'à m'en geler les mains
La forêt se laisse entendre, je n'en ai plus pour longtemps
Le vent me chavire, les branches me griffent profondément
Par désespoir, je creuse frénétiquement la terre,
Pour cette lueur, ce scintillement qui me fera oublier cette fatalité austère
Les ongles ternis par l'effort, je retrouve l'objet de mes pensées, de mes
    désirs les plus inavoués
Prise d'effroi, je réalise la détérioration de cette précieuse destinée
Autrefois rouge, maintenant noire
Autrefois résistante à la rouille, maintenant rongée par mes caprices
    aléatoires
Autrefois carrée
Maintenant ronde
Si seulement la clé était en ma possession, je voyagerais à travers le
    monde
Libérée de mes secrets bien gardés, bien scellés
Je pourrais remplacer ce gouffre frissonnant par des bijoux se baignant
Dans le doré
La sortie lumineuse m'attend
Le chronomètre s'est arrêté au bon moment
La forêt se referme, la boite s'évapore
Dans ma chambre il ne reste que ce reflet digne d'une métaphore
Encore, la clé est à chercher
Encore, la boite est à ouvrir
Mes angoisses seront-elles apaisées?
Pourrais-je enfin dormir sans m'évanouir ?

DISCOVERING WHAT LIES UNDER THESE TRAITS

Emotions
Such complex states of being
Some need to hide, others find the release so freeing
Neutral and steady
As a rock
What happened to get you in a state
Of shock
One drop of tear, the crowd gets agitated
Is it exhaustion or did this news get you heated?
The eye of the beholder senses this radar for weakness
Don't worry, some dust caused this constant bleakness
One ounce of anger
Suddenly people talk of liquor
Following the viciousness of a circle
This comment makes you bitter
Volcanoes erupting from inside
Cool and collected from the side
You see me glide
Your lack of sleep, the weather outside got you dried
You put on a fake smile and hope they don't crack past this barrier
At work, the casual talks get us through
But at home, under the covers at night, we got no choice but to turn
  blue

CŒUR DE MON ENFANCE,
CŒUR DE MES REPAS

Son habileté à tenir en un seul morceau
Sa ferme chair qui succombe au couteau
Ma surprise découverte quand je dispute le noyau
Sa verdure toute entière qui nous fait penser aux végétaux
Sa capacité à se dissimuler, à se fondre parmi les locaux
Fruit de mon enfance fruit
De mon existence
Avec toi, les coups sont oubliés,
Avec toi, la joie est retrouvée
Parfaitement symétrique, je me dois de te
Partager
Nos papilles gustatives étant réveillées, nos rires profonds sont
Dévoilés
En jours tristes comme en jours heureux, je peux toujours compter sur
    toi
Je n'ai qu'à fermer les yeux et imaginer ton joli minois
Je l'admets,
Jamais tu ne m'as déçu
J'ai pu être dotée d'un don pour choisir les perles parmi les déchus
Mais je crois surtout que tu ne me lâches point depuis le début

FARBERWARE

GRAY HAIR IN THE WHITE ROOM

Can you see that your hair has turned gray?
I noticed that your earthy curls have faded away
Can you sense those dry riddles, making course on my palm?
I have tried every cream to retard this feisty bomb
Can you feel time
Mocking us
Pushing us
All I want is to catch the right bus
At the end of the week with you
I want to watch the wheels turn and go back
With you, I want to be guided through a silent track
A white room
With no birds or grass
I want to know what happens when you let go of the glass
Enough of the clean cuts and pretty pictures
Let be, the mess of life comes to give me lectures
Let the crash bring me back to a time
A time
When numbers didn't hit so hard
A time when you stressed over picking the smallest card
Yes, we've slowed down
Yes, we've quit town
But when I look at you after this long marathon
Despite your back cracking and your cheekbones gone
The mirror of your soul hasn't changed a bit
All those years
The color has continued to sit
Every second they blink
I'm being reminded to hang on
So, don't you dare lie down on this lawn
Get up and stare those green eyes through
My soul
Don't let go of my gaze, fall into this hole
For I need us to walk to the white room
And be forever doomed
Doomed we didn't bloom

INCERTITUDE D'UNE DOULEUR SANS FIN

Je sens mon corps changer
Je ne sais rien des douleurs du bas
Tous les signes sont là
Je ne vais pas bien
Doutes du cerveau, foire à questions
Je me jette sur internet, que de directions
Le mental prend le dessus
La vérité est décousue
J'attends la venue du concret, qu'importe sa qualification
Dénotatif, connotatif, ce ne sont que degrés d'une solidification
Savoir que le malheur s'invite est bien triste
Mais ne pas se préparer à son arrivée nous lance dans le hors-piste
À avoir su, je ne me serais pas aventurée dans les bois
À avoir su, je me serais munie de deux skis adéquats
Me voilà à attendre que les bosses disparaissent
Me voilà à attendre que la température baisse
Un infini de mois sont passés
Aucune réponse de trouvée
Aucun antidote ne fera demi-tour
La vie reprendra son cours
Les cheveux perdus sous la douche
Maintenant je comprends que ce n'était qu'une retouche
Le cerveau persuadé d'une fatalité
Je me suis habituée à la nécessité
La nécessité de croire qu'une maladie approche
La nécessité de confronter une vérité atroce
Les démarches sont fortement présentes
Pourtant la réponse finale, incohérente
À jamais je vivrai dans l'incertitude
À jamais j'oublierai cette fausse exactitude

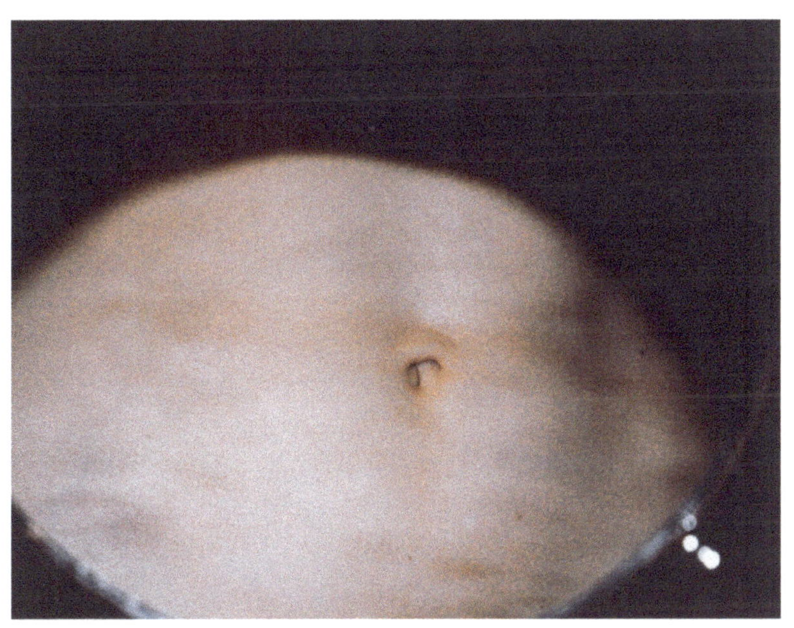

THE UNBORN

It would have spoken up in class
It would have played the bass
It would have gone to a wild festival
It would have gotten the right answer by the decimal
It would have dyed its hair blonde
It would have traveled far and beyond

It would have gained confidence with time
It would have enjoyed the rocky climb
It would have embraced its unconventional passions
It would have learned not to judge these violent reactions
It would have found life to be pretty messy and unfair
It would have loved to be quite unique and rare

It would have shown, rather than risk speaking to deceive
It would have taken on a new pair of eyes and quit being naive
It would have trusted its impulsions, let go of brain convulsions
It would have not cared in the long haul to not have won
It would have not feared having to catch the race
It would have utterly trusted in the universe
                remembering the possibility to traverse
It would have shaped its own opinions
It would have not let itself be manipulated like some unaware minion

It would have not cared in the long haul to not have won
It would have not feared having to catch the race

I'm sorry science has failed to make you be
After your liquid evaporated, there was me

UNOPENED PRESENT I CAN'T SEEM TO GIVE

Rumors have it
There is a gift waiting under the tree
365 days, bit by bit
And it still hasn't been opened, not even for tea
The wrapping paper smells like a relationship we never had
The postcard smells like a brutal accident that has made me sad
I wish I could give it to you
One phone call and the tree would go to waste
We don't know each other yet, but I already believe the will in overcoming
    being erased
You see
I think about you more often than anybody might think
I am aware of the painful solitude and of the fear that we might all need
    a shrink
Damage has been done
This gift has been meticulously put together in a miracle
The gestures of a surgeon, tape that wouldn't for a soul let go of this
    resilient material
These moonlights
Have been waiting for you; an awareness of what you might do next
Remember when we used to be kids
How communication was already so complex
You hated me for the attention I was given
You feared rejection
Being unprepared for this passive aggressiveness
I looked up to you and your biggest aspiration
To me, this dream was enough,
To you, nothing would ever be enough
I wish I had the words to articulate the immensity of my anger and sadness
But all I can do for now is keep this unopened present, this gladness
For the day will come when the ribbons can be unmade
And the discussion storm
out of the norm
We might be far from each other, common blood runs through the veins
Am I sick of playing games, of secretly giving you names!
You are kind, you have to let me see
I am lost, you have to help me be

THE CHASE OF AN UNSATISFACTORY RUN

Since day one, you wanted this piece
Of jewelry
Ignoring all your needs, you were obsessed with the nudity
You chased it across boulevards, ready to pass through the red lights
You could only see below your belly button, no surprise you didn't
    know
Her rights
Driven by an obsessive need for completion, you knew of no center
    position
Either nothing
Either you could feel her breasts
Either everything
Either you left
No is not an answer
As a man, you have been taught to never give up the pace
Never surrender
You kept your breath and testosterone well in place
No problem if you have offended
Her
You are convinced she's reciprocating
Among the negative results, there has to be hope
You kept on pulling up to this street, craving to confuse this smooth
    mist for toxic dope
You learned every single piece that composes her life
Listened to every crumb just so
You could act dumb
Congratulations, you've reached the next level
The city has been evacuated
Now that you've entered the lagoon, you are disgusted you've even
    waited
The chase is over, and so is
The desire
The fire has been put out; all that is left is
This compulsive liar
But don't you worry
The lagoon is filled with brand-new shiny stones
Be ready to catch some, be as good as Sherlock Holmes
Be aware of crocodiles
They bite hard and leave you to suffer in piles
You may have broken a lot of pendants already,
But the rings have perceived you as sneaky, as unsteady

Don't come back to the previous level when you have no one to marry
The chase is over, you have no oxygen left
I suggest you go home and
Take a minute to rest
Running is so overrated
Trust me, go on a walk with a compass and get yourself oriented
To the North is accepting defeat
To the South is considering retreat
To the West is listening to her heartbeat
To the East is not having to repeat
Well, I guess now you must have fallen asleep

WORDS OF THE WORLD

Words, components of a universe that attract
Fascination
Elocution, people admire this gift
Pieces of letter forming an intention
This invisible manifesto that smells of communication
And yet, people choose to lock up the meaning, beat up
The language
They would rather use an expressive silence to their advantage
The thing is, they find it hard to choose between
Billions of combinations
Combinations of billions
The right way to compose significant declarations
I will give it to you
Ordering up your burger can be made with easy vigor
But how about when it's time to inform your patient of an existing
    tumor
Sometimes, the most poignant speeches can only meet you halfway
Sometimes
Words can only make an unnecessary disarray
In hard times
A wink, a smile, a hug is all you can deal with
Because truly an overwhelming letter is this crude reminder of the pith
When words keep disappointing our needs
We have to turn our heads toward gestures
Gestures of hate, gestures of love, sometimes filled
In uneven measures
A heart is bloody
Mountains are peaky, no matter the country
No matter the term
Don't let them squirm
Hold on to the words unexpressed, keep them still
For when you'll be holding the right dictionary
For when you'll cease spilling your guts in a hurry
You'll find the right formula
The one attached to your internal orchestra
You'll let the melody play even before you've shown the audience
Your saxophone
Trust me, you'll never want this clarity to embody the wrong tone
You cannot define the state you're in, you say?

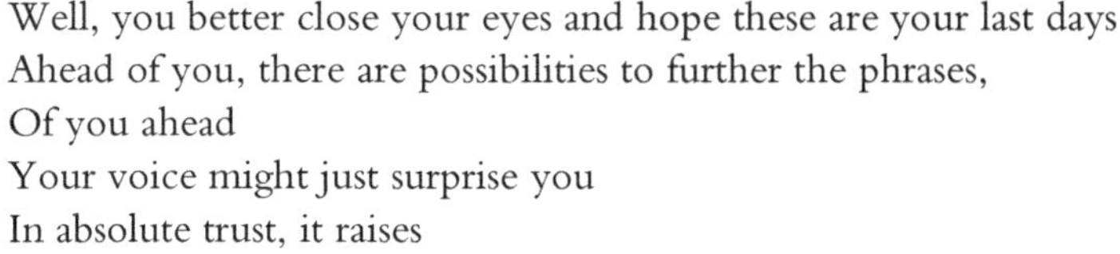

Well, you better close your eyes and hope these are your last days
Ahead of you, there are possibilities to further the phrases,
Of you ahead
Your voice might just surprise you
In absolute trust, it raises

No picture could ever describe the power of words

DÉSERT DU QUARTIER 19

La peur dystopienne nous a aveuglés
Les rues sont désormais
Désertes
On n'est pas dans le far West
On n'est pas sur le point de faire une découverte
La soirée est laissée à elle-même
Aucun bruit
Aucune distraction
Reine de son empire, elle observe les pions se faire prendre des contraventions
Hélicoptères en cavale, sirènes d'alarme mises en place
Je comprends bien que tout le monde se cache
Que personne ne veut faire face
Notre liberté
Réduite, ce n'est plus qu'une simple question de sécurité
Un système, un régime oppressif, on le voit tranquillement apparaître
    dans cette obscurité
Au grand jour, les foules pourraient encore frapper, réclamer le bon sens
Alors qu'en pleine nuit, seuls les ratons laveurs savent monter en puissance
Le tunnel est toujours en construction
La circulation mise à néant
La ville doit bien se moquer de nous
Nous prendre pour de sacrés fainéants
Il est vrai
Nous restons en retrait
Bien sages à obéir tels des soldats
Mais qu'avons-nous à gagner, à nous lever et réagir, aussi vite on
    retombe bien bas
L'impasse est grande
On ne peut plus continuer
Il faut stagner
On se souviendra de cette soumission
On se souviendra de cet abandon
En ce moment
On a peur de se révolter
Guidés par des idéologies bien controversées
En ce moment
On donne une confiance aveugle à ceux qui suent de gouverner
Quand ça sera fini
On ne prendra plus pour acquis nos droits
On redéfinira la déontologie
Ce n'est pas parce que Kant a parlé de l'obéissance absolue qu'on ne
    peut point changer de philosophie
Quand ça sera fini

Il faudra remettre en question les infrastructures, les mentalités
Ce n'est pas parce qu'un étranger s'est infiltré dans nos vies qu'il faut
   mythifier le passé, qu'il faut magnifier ce qui auparavant existait
On s'adapte à une catastrophe
Strophe
Ne pensez-vous pas qu'on voit maintenant clairement les fondations de
   notre société ?
Cette période nous empêche d'agir, mais notre pensée continue de circuler
Les règles sont certes établies
Pour nous éviter l'anarchie
Nous guider vers le droit chemin
Mais ces paroles vides de sens et ces écrits lâches définissent notre monde
   de demain
On s'empresse de courir vers une fin, vers la disparition de cet étranger
Alors qu'on n'est pas prêt à faire face à ce qui nous arrivera, quand on
   sera de nouveau étranglés
On a déjà hâte de voir la fin
Pensant que les problèmes partiront avec
Et pourtant, ils existaient déjà bien avant qu'un ennemi commun
Vienne envahir notre planète

UN CONCRET, UNE ABSTRACTION

Cher Monsieur, vous êtes là à porter votre sarreau
À vous tenir à carreau
Chère Madame, vous êtes là à tenir votre plume
À vous imaginer dans les bras de Neptune

Au collège, la différence les concernait
Cette incompréhension les tourmentait
Les chiffres, les solutions lui permettent de
Comprendre le monde avec sagesse
Les possibilités, l'évasion lui permettent de
Croire en l'éclosion d'un monde romanesque
Elle passe souvent à côté du concret,
Volontairement elle lui tourne le dos
Il sait que l'abstraction l'observe avec fermeté
D'en haut
Il ferme le rideau
Cette manière de suivre sans scrupules son intuition autrefois l'agaçait
Autrefois, cette appréhension à croire à l'inexplicable la ravageait
Jamais il ne se laisse guider par de fortes impulsions
Des sensations
Inconfortables
Jamais, elle ne se laisse enraciner par des savoirs
Des incontournables
En temps de jeunesse
Les contraires s'attirent, les corps se confondent
Les esprits restent, à l'appel les différences répondent
En temps de vieillesse
Ce jeune homme s'est laissé emporter
Par cette spontanéité contagieuse
Avec le temps, il a vite compris que sa placidité
Mettait ombrage sur cette audacieuse
Cette jeune femme s'est vu admirer un génie incompris
Froid plein de sang-froid
Avec le temps, elle a vite compris
Que son amertume est à l'égal du héros de Casablanca
Entre les écrits idéalistes et les thèses scientifiques
Une hiérarchie naturelle s'est immiscée
Il est clair, le vieil homme se croit plus important, sa carrière est divinisée
Des recherches abouties, des médicaments mis sur le marché
En effet
Le concret évolue et gagne des places à s'en arracher
Des perles sorties de l'imagination, des créations fictives, des dédicaces

En effet

L'abstraction est mise à la cave, tranquillement elle est vue comme une
    disgrâce

Sa femme a du talent, il a un déni saillant

Son mari est connu aux yeux de l'univers

Elle perd espoir en son domaine minoritaire

Si seulement ils pouvaient réaliser

Qu'ils ont besoin l'un de l'autre

Les extrêmes n'ont pas à s'ignorer

La symbiose peut suivre la marée haute

Aidez Madame à ne pas trop s'envoler

À garder un pied sur terre

Aidez Monsieur à éviter de trop suivre les critères

À sentir les fouets du vent, de l'air

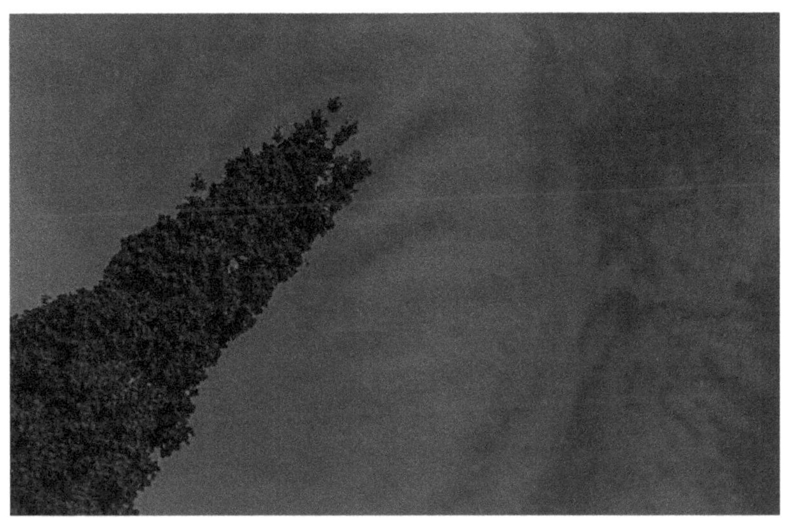

A DEDICATION TO YOU, MY READER

I have had enough of the numerated excuses, of this never-ending
    procrastination
Only did I need an assignment to let myself write; well I couldn't let rot
    inside this narration
This voice would not have gained value if spoken, only put in verses
    can it awaken the senses
I spent so much time on these words, on perfecting the rhymes, on the
    meaning behind the tenses
Late at night, waiting for the brain to work in a crude emptiness, to let
    the matters be poignant
Shaking at the idea of criticism, of this piece being the fruit of disappointment
I used to read the most impressive poems, admiring the complexity it
    takes to amaze through pieces of paper
In immersing myself in the enumerations and metaphors of Baudelaire, I
    found it safer
No confrontations, no expectations, a final product that is handed to
    you
Now I have to envision you in your bed, having a peek inside my brain,
    critiquing the view
I always perceived the act of composing as private
But soon enough after you buy a car, you eventually have to drive it
I don't know your story; I don't know what brings you to this very
    collection
But I trust you in taking care of my work, whether it is of affection or
    disconnection
My part here has been completed, no more modifications allowed, no
    more readings done out loud
Whatever baggage you come with, whatever interpretations you put on
    the board
Thank you for taking the time to read the core of my thinking, to cross
    this border unexplored
If it weren't for you, these segments of my expression would have left
    a prude
You are the reason the energy keeps burning, the letters consumed, the
    soul and mind renewed
You may have been mistaken; I didn't plan to only write for the author
At the end of the day, it is the reader I truly want to value and honor
This is a message for the beholder of my precious, to never let go of the
    projects, might they be perceived as too ambitious

You are the protagonist of your life, make it your own, note down the
    novel through the doubts and the questions
Let the pencil flow, let it guide you to the many directions
You can be the writer of your journey,
Don't yet stop at the first village so cold and blurry
The bumps on the road are what make accomplishment so gratifying
    and worthy

DROP ON THE FLOOR

Life cannot be scripted
Mundane moments don't guide you toward the purchase of a ticket
When sad scenes arise, in your mind they persist but the actors have
    already moved on
Spontaneity is fabricated, reactions simulated, the artifice of it all is a
    pure phenomenon
When a woman cries on the bus
Onscreen, the passengers have to seem compassionate
When I saw a woman cry on the bus
Nobody budged, the lack of activism was disproportionate
I could not believe my eyes, I searched around for the director
One minute that I dared to look away from my phone, I caught a unique
    time-lapse enter
A stranger in who for a second felt this public place to be receptive of
    her burden
You could already tell from the minute she held the helm so tight that
    her strength would not win over this constant hurting
In vain she had to drop the curtain
Just like a memorable laugh can be heard through sirens
Sad eyes do not lie, they make you wish you were floating alone on an
    island
I assume she thought she was discreet
When she looked over her shoulder after wiping her tears in heat
I assume she thought she had made a bad impression
When she quickly glanced at her reflection
An image that she seemed to want to forget
A recall of the distressing resent
I assume she didn't notice my presence, admiring all her gestures
Or else she wouldn't have borne this satisfactory smile before leaving as
    light as feathers
I had just witnessed the main character, determined and strong-willed
A cinematic enigma presenting humanity in its purest form, the one that
    gets its plot fulfilled
If the other passengers would have stopped at the right time, a perfect
    moment of unity
They would have observed the brutality behind vulnerability
This woman, by the hero of the story didn't need to be saved
Nor did she need to be reassured
She knew of the outcomes, of how she could be treated, she chose not
    to let them win
In the reality of it all, she voluntarily let out the emotion as quickly as
    she took it back in

Maybe she received a text that saddened her universe, maybe she traveled
   out in one of her anterior memories, tasted a piece of nostalgia
She had it neat and complete when entered, and when time to let go,
   she put it back together and acted as an alpha
Forever I'll keep in mind this experience that left me in wonder
Because next time, maybe I'll choose to step up and throw the
   indifference in a dumper
I could have simply offered an ear to share her sorrow
I could have simply let her know
Of my arms, of how they could be borrowed
But I will never know
What she truly needed

As such, not everyone envies sharing a private thing
As such, some people prefer to keep it under their skin

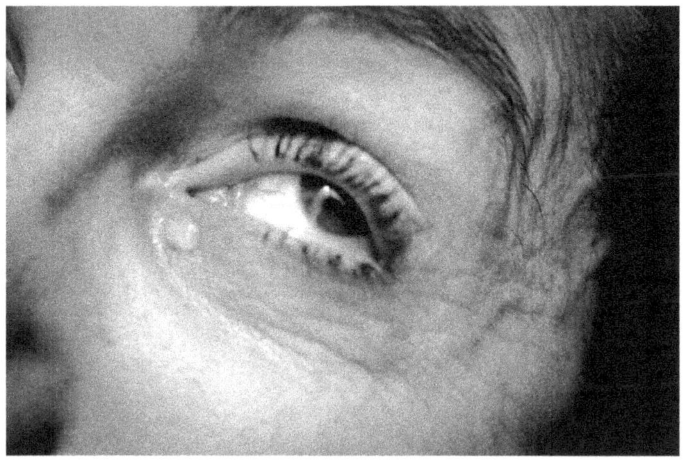

PASSER À L'ÉCRAN SANS GLAMOUR

Mon prénom est réduit à une simple banalité
Plus aucun effort pour le prononcer à ma façon
Mon nom de famille n'a plus le privilège d'être réservé
Pour les intimes, il est arrivé à se caser à la première place du wagon
Les murs familiers de ma chambre se sentent observés, par des étrangers,
    par des vignettes mélangées
Ma voix soudainement contrôlée
Mes opinions doivent attendre avant de pouvoir gagner de la valeur
Je projette une facette loin du toucher
Loin des rumeurs
Je passe à l'écran devant tant
Je suis réduite à des raclements
Expressions faciales
D'approbation et pouces en l'air
Seulement, j'aimerais bien que l'on connaisse mon odeur
Mes peurs
Que mon corps ne passe pas à côté de cette carrière
Prise entre ces barreaux magnétiques
Je me prends à vouloir hurler à
Vouloir partager l'agacement qui vient avec l'incompréhension
Entre les fichiers à télécharger et les power point à déceler, seul le réel
    nous ramène à l'unique précision
Alors que je suis à l'avant d'un voilier à naviguer avec tout l'équipement
    nécessaire
Je panique à l'idée de voyager seule, étant face à la mer comme seule
    adversaire
Les mots ont beau
Rassurer
Les promesses ont beau
Faire rêver

Je ne suis qu'un grain de riz dans une casserole
Que la radio cassée d'une bagnole
Il pourrait n'avoir jamais atteint l'assiette
Ce n'est pas sans lui qu'on va s'inquiéter de conduire sans cassette
Si je disparais soudainement du carré, l'on suppose que j'ai abandonné la
    séance

On ne me voit plus, en réalité je suis tombée bêtement sur le dos, ma
    foi sans élégance
J'attends la venue de possibles éclatements de rire qui pourraient remplir
    la gêne d'une douleur qui réveille l'esprit
Les impulsions du moment n'arrivent pas encore à passer à l'écran
À parcourir ce périmètre décent
Mon absence ne cause aucun soupçon, aucunes inquiétudes ne se font
Comme si de rien était je me rattache à cette étiquette collée
Je veux te voir danser librement sur une tonalité saccadée
Je veux te voir pousser un cri surprenant que le micro n'a pas encore
    eu la chance de capter
Je veux savoir si tu préfères porter des souliers confortables
Des leggings bien relâchés
Ou bien des bottes à en donner des chevilles mémorables
Des jeans bien serrés
Mais pour l'instant je suis coincée, le digital nous sépare, loin de toi, j'essaie
    de voir ce qui te tourmente, ce qui t'habite quotidiennement
Néanmoins, on ne se contacte que pour discuter des heures de rassemblements
Du moment où l'on passera à la télévision

Le temps écoulé
Les salles réduites à un chronomètre ajusté
Nos supérieurs manipulant la télécommande sans vision
Nos mots coupés
Nos gestes réduits à néant, je n'ai même pas eu le temps de placer
Un point à ma phrase
Je n'ai pas vérifié la netteté de l'image
La couronne revient aux satellites, aux réseaux, aux connexions
Humaines sont-elles ces connections ?
Je pourrais rester à dormir, m'enfuir de ce partage superficiel, matriciel
Je pourrais décider d'hiberner, le temps de retourner à de réelles performances
    shakespeariennes
Mais cela voudrait dire que la bagnole cassée ne s'est pas laissée être
    réparer
Qu'elle a attendu avant de reprendre ce chemin connu aux yeux de
    tous, ce sentier dégagé
Je ne suis pas la seule à passer à l'écran
Je ne suis pas la seule, maintenant je m'en rends compte, à visionner ce
    passage de vie comme inquiétant

Il faut se coller aux autres grains de riz
Pour faire de merveilleux sushis
Il faut ne pas oublier que les autres vignettes ne portent plus le nom de
    fictives
Que sous les pouces en l'air établis
À la surface
En profondeur,
Bouillent des navigateurs
Qui sont submergés par les mêmes soucis

FORBIDDEN FRUIT

Right behind the transparency
Looking up to the sky, I came across an apple untouched
Not being able to move, I watched closely
As the lights burned down, as the door slowly clutched
From the alley, next to the trash can, all I aspired to do was breathe
    better
And yet the big guys upstairs took oxygen for granted
As I jumped up on the stool, as I struggled in peeking at the interior,
    my spirit was disenchanted
All that remained were dying plants and a source of vitamin neglected
Such careful and fragile elements merely
Sat there to provide evidence of a specific behavior, of being socially
Connected
They want to prone Organic, as it speaks for a truthful and secure
    environment
My ass, these corporate offices sit at the top of the chain for the gratifying
    hunt
The apple was only there for decoration, I would have bet you with
    time the color would have remained intact
That is if I took a bite, the skin wouldn't peel
Off, the juice wouldn't spill
Down, and that my teeth would have hit hard from confusing reality
    to its correspondent Artifact
Except, the more I looked at it
The more I wanted to believe that by resting on the concrete
It didn't fulfill its only function
And that by not having eaten in days, chance had found me, had made
    me look, made me wonder of the veracity of this conjunction
I could not imagine
How this person could have left this treasure behind
I could not imagine
I was about to break through this unreachable space, therefore putting
    all the social differences aside
As my appetite grew stronger and my hands were getting closer to the
    forbidden fruit
Not any other substitute
I pictured a silhouette coming back
In exhaustion, hoping to capture her kid's snack
I suddenly remembered my mother and how much effort she used to
    put into selecting the proper subsistence

How a simple bag of grapes made me feel wanted, cherished, and in this
    absolute second washed away angriness that comes with this mean
    existence
It had accidentally been forgotten, what if
By appeasing my hunger, my own needs, what if
I caused the misfortune of this unseen form, this outlined figure
What if she barely made it home with enough money to feed her only
    family, supposing there's a missing mister
This apple might have seemed a simple purchase for the cashier, but
    for me it was more than I could ever handle in one day
And despite the weakness of my bones, the frequency
Of my migraines, here I was weighing my options, acknowledging
The lack of courtesy I might display?
If I had left by mistake a possession of mine, would that woman have
    gone through the same process?
I just assumed she would not budge given the opportunity, as long as
    she's making Progress
As long as she's winning
At chess
Because let's face the facts
Forget tact
I could never move until my life is in danger
While she's the real game changer
So, as you would have probably guessed by now, I threw the stool at
    this fragile transparency and took the matter in my own hands
You can call me a thief
You can curse at me
Judge me
But remember, this is only a story
It never existed, but as you're reading, you're suddenly aware of the
    beauty
The beauty there is in the accessibility
That if one day, all your material goods disappeared from your space
You would risk breaking the fabricated law and throw the moral
    obligations in its face

THE TREE OF SATISFACTION

It has come to my attention you beg for more, that your knowledge
    has not survived past the expiration date
The time has arrived to exceed the bare minimum, to set your vision
    straight
You shaped this long neck of yours, you practiced the mobility of your
    articulations
Before working on the brain, you needed to review the principles of
    the body, the indisputable foundations
The greasy mark of a knuckle on your cheek, you get up despite the
    bruises, there is no one to get yourself recovered
Your surroundings have left the battle, you will have to settle down the
    voices, to get the trauma smothered
No more laying on the scratchy grass at noon
No more seeking different angles and shapes of the moon
Remember the nasty dreams that have you all curled up like a spoon
The night is only there for you to sleep
The broad daylight is of no use if it is dizziness and vertigo you want
    to keep
To reach an impression of finality
You need to get to the top of this tree
Grab the farthest apple of them all
To reach a sense of relief, you need
To bite into this crunchy texture, feel
The juicy elixir invade your organism, make its way into the hall
You won't get immortal
Don't let the expectations speak, it is not asked of us to confront evolution,
    birth and destruction all bottled up in a circle
You have been warned, it is quite temporary, the feeling will leave in
    a matter of an instance
You may be strong and agile, I advise you to jump before the conifer
    destructs the effect of the molecules, of this untested substance
You have built yourself up to the top of the branches
Observe now how the ground is filled with ashes
Ashes in which you land, blend
Ashes that used to make you tired of the trials, the errors, and the
    deception
Ashes that led you to taste the liquid of a complete satisfaction
The tree has disappeared, the elixir evaporated in the atmosphere
I know you wanted to stay up here
To not make an effort anymore
But with time, you'll be disgusted in losing the touch of the ground, the
    beauty there is feeling your knees sore

Drinking up elixirs will only bring deception, a rollercoaster between
    curiosity for big apples and taking
The small ones for granted
When you have nowhere else to look, you lose track of the genius there
    is in the slanted
You see, it's quite dangerous to already perceive ahead of you
The end of a journey
A car accident can be predicted when you
Follow the lines of a snaky route, of the curvy

L'ŒIL QUI GUETTE

Tant que tu continueras à m'observer
Je ne pourrais plus bouger
Pas même d'un pouce
Tes faits et gestes m'animent, à chaque mouvement brusque
Je me rappelle de ta nature autrefois douce
Avec tes yeux de félin qui traquent chaque recoin d'une pièce, je me
    sens comme une gazelle
Trop peu pour moi la chasse, trop peu pour moi l'attente cruauté, en
    retrait j'attends de m'enfuir et d'éviter cette tuerie solennelle
Le fait est, à travers les herbes hautes, je n'arrive guère à distinguer
Tes traits
Surnaturelle ou réelle
Ta forme, ton apparence est la cause de mon insomnie, de ma colère
    interne qui n'attend que de se relâcher
De sacrer
Quoi que je fasse
Je perds d'avance pendant que tu ricanes entre la fragilité de tes moustaches
Entre la densité de tes crocs
Tu te crois bien fort à ne me laisser aucune porte de sortie, à faire de
    moi l'escroc
Et je sais que même si je te lance des yeux nus, que je te laisse expérimenter
    le déchirement auquel j'ai dû
Faire face avant d'avoir croisé ton pelage
Tu t'en prendras à une autre, tu feras d'elle un tas d'os perdu
Au milieu des feuillages
J'ai un choix à faire, une possibilité à bâcler, la nécessité de m'agripper
En celle que je peux croire bonne
Mais voilà
J'ai longtemps pesé le pour et contre, et je dois dire qu'aucune n'arrivera
À calmer la colère qui harponne
Habitée par ton imposante stature, tu m'as fait croire que les dés avaient
    été lancés
Que jamais les rôles ne pourraient s'inverser
Si je suis encore vivante, c'est bien parce que ma valeur a été réduite à
    ma capacité d'atteindre la flotte avant ton estomac déjà trop plein
Si je reste à ne rien faire, c'est bien parce que j'ai été faite victime et toi
    un sacré vilain
Je ne suis qu'élégance et longévité
Tu n'es que défiance et brutalité
Je suis destinée à danser parmi les plus grands palais
Tu es destiné à te battre dans les grands matchs de boxe, jusqu'à la
    dernière goutte à suer
Mon corps long et fin, mes pas soignés et gracieux, mes cornes qui me
    servent de chapeau, mes beaux yeux qui masquent mes intentions

Tes muscles saillants, tes pas à la fois fougueux à la fois si minutieusement
    calculés, ta chevelure qui en dit long sur tes ambitions
Jamais je n'oserais
Prétendre pouvoir te battre en duel, tes griffes me couperaient
Le souffle en une minute
Jamais tu n'oserais
Prétendre être aussi vif, dynamique et futé que moi, je pourrais
Monter un coup bien pensé
En une minute
Remarque comme je me balade jamais seule, que cette boule qui te sert
    de tête est assez creuse, que la précaution reste en altitude
Remarque comme la distraction peut arriver à tes fins, je me faufile derrière
    toi pendant que ma partenaire semble souffrir, pendant qu'elle simule
    une certaine attitude
Remarque comme le vent est mon ultime allié
Il vient de frapper ta chevelure de plein fouet
Maintenant je peux annoncer à la savane qu'un coup de poignard a été
    lancé
Oui, pendant que tu avais le dos tourné
Le roi est rendu aveugle, nous épargnant ce regard si dur
Le roi ne pourra plus décider de notre sort, que nos gestes soient vus
    comme purs ou impurs
Nous sommes finalement libres de cette dictature

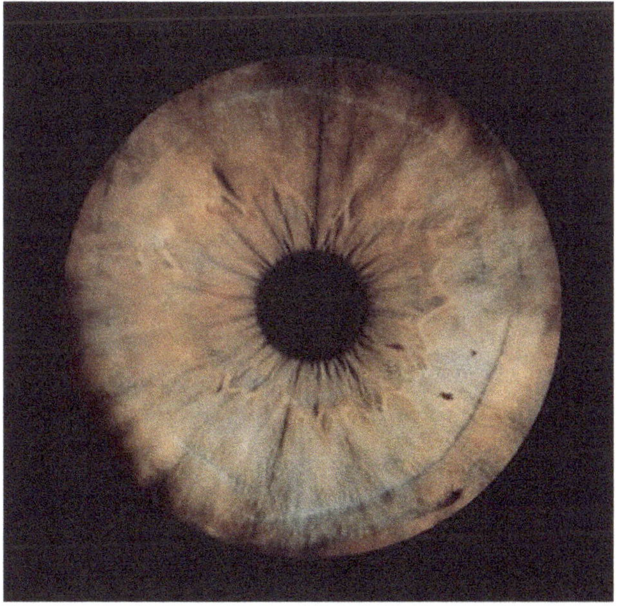

ABSTINENCE KEEPS US FROM MOVING

Listening to John Cage has made us feel like fools, we kept waiting for
something to lift us from the edge of our seat
No particular sounds were expressed, no work was put into the hearing
of a piece of music that contained the pattern of a beat
The piano stood at the center; the keys untouched kept us mindful of
pure silence
There we pioneered abstinence of content, between the controlled and
the unexpected there wasn't any balance
From the breaths and gulps merely perceived to the actual artistic
performance
Confrontation to the mundane and the uneventful began to question
our conformance
In our usual, silence is where nothing extraordinary happens, it is
The hint of a boring moment
When really it is
In choosing to avoid that we deprive ourselves of this underrated endowment
We keep running away from the discomfort it procures, as if filling in
the space would be more valuable than letting things flow
We are scared of what we might discover if conversations run out of
time, if emptiness becomes the main character of the talk show
But if we choose to mute ourselves and to perceive quietness
as simply depicting the normal
The new paranormal
becomes birds singing
Leaves swinging
Feet stomping
In a way, silence doesn't exist, it is only subjective to those who decide
to make it count
In a way, a complex word isn't always understood, it is only attainable
to those who search at the fount
I heard people say friendship is tested by the capacity of communicating
in wordless exchanges
Just like the greatness of an essay doesn't reduce itself to the number of
pages
Without any pressure, see how the world in its smallness has a lot to
convey
Listen again to the immobile hands laying across the instrument, and see
how they slip away
It is not because you cannot see that the masquerade hasn't set foot at
the rear end
That you need to set in advance your demands
Quite frankly it is better to wait than to pretend
Lack of magnitude only defines the contour of the usual that resonates

If you let the expectations of a greater moment invade your vision,
    abstinence will rise up and let you know of the ways she dominates
Sufficiency is only overlooked if it is more
We look and ask for
If you wind up in the alley of a Saturday night, abstinence will make
    you realize you've stopped keeping count of the score

83

ON THE SURFACE OF YOUR PHONE

It is easier to stay on the surface, floating above reality
It is alluring to rub out a crooked structure, trading
Authenticity for a rhinoplasty
For one day, a filter is all it takes for the compliments to rush back on
    a profile
So edited, so well naturally constructed, the hours spent to be in sync
    with the latest lifestyle
Either coffee either
Tea
Such depthless dispositions
If it is not to show an underworld, what is the exact mission
What is captured stands for a performance, a performance of imitation
Just like a director won't allow for the only take to be the product
    advertised
This account is overflowed with portraits that have you mesmerized
Only, the actors had to get better at repeating the same text
In reaching the unity of intention and subtext
Only, the one you keep zooming in on at the tip of your fingers had
    behind her hours of
readjusting the angles, eyes and eyebrows flexed
You were contempt of your forty likes, glorifying the picture you
    took at your mom's
The surface keeps outnumbering, promoting a bunch of skin creams
    and lip balms
Funny thing is, the algorithm won't let this icon consider you
While thanks to your wiliness to consume, the hydration of your lips
    has produced the savings of a bank, shiny and new
Think about the energy of a body all channeled to film an egocentric
    short video that doesn't rhyme with usefully
Think about the last day you've slept, the last day you haven't studied
    for the chance of an opportunity
On the surface, the waves seem to have missed hours of a bad weather
    outcome
But just touch the edges of water, how it is inaccessible, how it makes
    you feel empty, useless, non-existent
Don't let one sunny day block your common sense, a digital story that
    makes your depression more insistent
Once those books have met the gaze of a garbage can
Once your days are reduced to getting sessions of fake tan
You might inspire a lot; you might get your name registered in our
    brains
But once you've started, there is no going back, your career launched,
    there is no space for playing games

We expect to see content to amuse our lives, we expect to have some
    films for which we can feed you remarks
From you're a slut to you're a queen, there are no borders, on the
    surface no limits, below plenty of sparks
And don't come back pretending your sadness has not been warned
Don't come back hating on us while you're in Dubai and we're barely
    paying the bills
Living in a building we have now scorned
Thanks to you, I envy the colors that don't exist
Thanks to you, I envy the mountains that I haven't yet kissed

LA VIE APRÈS L'ESSOUFFLEMENT

La médecine ne ment pas, les battements ont cessé de semer l'ordre

Les couleurs ont fané, seul le bleu magistral est perceptible dans la morgue

Une suite de corps ayant perdu leurs vitaux, une identité volée par cette entité

Celle qu'on craint toute notre vie, celle qui arrive quand on a enfin valorisé la mortalité

Un à un, on les voit disparaître, on est certain que parce qu'on ne peut plus discerner

Leur présence n'est plus d'actualité

Leur souffle ne coure plus dans les rues

Mais j'aime à croire que l'objet n'est pas tombé par hasard, que la gravité n'est pas le seul intrus

Je voudrais bien ranger cette réflexion au placard mais il déborde déjà trop de questions, de remords et de croyances

Je voudrais bien la confier à un proche mais je crains une possible arrogante nonchalance

On m'a appris devant le grand tableau blanc que les corps périssaient

Se décomposaient

Que l'antonyme de l'existence se réduisait à la projection d'un météore

Mais par-delà ce cratère doit bien rester des particules dont le vide a fait son décor

Oui, un cœur cesse de battre mais qu'en est-il de l'inexplicable, de l'essence qu'on ne peut aspirer, retirer par la déclaration haute d'un être inanimé

Je ne prétends pas détenir la vérité, je veux simplement amener à décortiquer

Détacher le biscuit de l'exactitude de ses pépites d'hypothèses

Après l'essoufflement et l'usure d'une vie bien longue, comment peut-on être jugé dans le jardin du ciel de notre nature bonne ou mauvaise

Entre un cheminement sans entraves et quelques coups d'adultère

À qui réserve-t-on le droit d'envoyer l'un des deux à la source des flammes

J'aime à croire que chacun est renvoyé au début du cercle, et que ce souffle vital, on le soigne

J'aime à croire que le bébé qui nait à l'instant aura une vieille âme, que la destruction d'un corps aura permis l'éclosion d'un nouveau

Je me souviens de ces impressions de déjà vu

Comme la première fois que j'ai lu Hugo

J'ai cru à un disfonctionnement qui m'était dû

À une répétition de la même page, qu'importe le studio, qu'importe les sections

Mais avec du recul, je pense avoir vu des mémoires

Appartenant à une forme céleste, elle ne voulait que perturber le naturel,
    se faire savoir
Je ne suis pas folle, j'ai seulement des doutes sur ce qui vient après
    l'anéantissement
Je m'accroche au sensé nuit et jours, à faire aveuglément confiance à mon
    ouïe, à la dextérité de mon toucher, à cet instinct constant
En espérant de ne jamais m'agripper à l'impossible, de ne jamais
    entendre une voix à laquelle se rattacherait l'invalide
Car cela voudrait dire qu'on pourrait désormais grimper dans un arbre
    lors d'un orage torride

POUR UN AMI QUI A VU
LA CIGARETTE S'ÉTEINDRE

On m'a annoncé la triste nouvelle, une réalité qui fait réaliser
Que ça n'arrive pas qu'aux inconnus
La grande faux a encore frappé
Sans avertissement, comme lorsque les pluies arrivent alors qu'on avait
    annoncé
Un beau temps en continu
Cher ami, j'imagine bien que tu as peur
Que la possibilité de toucher se réduise en vapeur
Que les mois se transforment en secondes
Que la couleur de ses yeux fonde
Peut-être auras-tu voulu ne jamais l'avoir su?
L'attente d'une tragédie est plus pénible
Que d'arriver seulement au dernier acte, là où se dénoue le crédible
Mais, en soit, tu peux profiter
Tu peux compter
Tu peux tout donner
Au lieu de prendre pour acquis le spectacle, tu peux rester et en avoir le
    souffle coupé
Parce que dans ces moments durs, on met de côté sa fierté
Nos priorités autrefois considérées
Comme plus importantes
Par la consternation en cette période habitée,
Les batailles de jeunesse et les tensions partent dans une poussière tordante
De penser qu'un jour, on a vu le drame dans l'énervement que cette
    personne nous faisait ressentir
Et que maintenant, les fades sourires et la fragilité d'une maladie nous
    mettent hors de nous, nous font rebondir
C'est une lutte d'une immensité qu'on ne peut imaginer
Et tu dois te rassurer en te disant
Que c'est en donnant
Chaleur et soutien que l'esprit reprend de la ténacité
Quoiqu'il arrive, qu'importe la tournure des évènements
La faux n'arrivera jamais à détruire les sentiments
La place qu'ils possèdent dans ton cœur
Au travers de la destruction, du vide, crois au fait que c'est toi le seul
    vrai grimpeur

THE SMALLER AND BIGGER THINGS

The sound of the rain pouring on my soul
The liquid making me whole
The resting of my body frozen to death
The hesitation of my mind's breath
The fur so soft gliding through particles of skin
The red hat leading you to spin
The screams easier said than done
Misery wondering how it can be undone
The speed of an uncontrollable love
How easy it is to put on a pair of gloves
The shivers of a gentle touch
Catching the moon is asking for too much
The eyes closing to the ugly truth
Puzzles walking around the telephone booth
The force of the wind making you feel small
Choosing to finally cross the wall
The psychological cutting through the veins
The nostalgia of meeting you in trains
The tightness of clothes in the alley
Running away from war in a magical valley
The gasp of shock thrown away in the river
The emotions we never could deliver
The fish that jumps high to whisper
The gracious neck that remembered the heavy blister
The forest containing creature's revelations
The vibration there is in having a destination
The fragility of a canvas without any textures
The vulnerability hiding behind gestures
The bark of your demons floating in suspension
The nights of a true apprehended tension
The whiteness of buried lies
The black cat turning back to stare at you smiling in disguise
The damaged vessels of your pumping machine
Envying people that have already seen
The burning fire of an unwanted existence
Forgetting to measure the longest distance
The scrunching of the nose in complete silence
Staying away from the shallow balance
The weight of your laugh in the room,

The mirror that hasn't yet told you to bloom
The sleepless universe that exists on your lips
Exchanges that weren't part of the scripts
The poem without a name to be referred to
Sitting up from the overwhelming worldview
 that makes you you

LE DESTIN QUI TRANCHE

Rassurés par ce mot si facilement utilisé
Nous avons oublié ce qu'est de bousculer
À penser que nos mains tracent les lignes en l'absence de notre contrôle
Nous avons oublié de lui tourner le dos
Attirés par une fatalité déjà tracée, nos choix font figure de décorations
    en trop
Celles qu'on a placés avant d'avoir réalisé que rien ne tiendra
Les ficelles ne peuvent supporter ce poids
Placés à une certaine distance de nos défaites, nous attendons le moment
    décisif
Celui qui aura rendu cette traversée moins chaude, moins à vif
Les victoires ne sont plus gratifiantes
Les défaites sont la source d'une fée souffrante
Le présent ne sert à rien si dans le ciel
Le destin s'est chargé d'engager un chirurgien
Des cicatrices déjà dessinées
Des opérations casées
La géométrie des incisions calculés avec ardeur
Le futur baille sur sa chaise en attendant d'appuyer
Sur le bon bouton, à ne pas se tromper
Entre un docteur et un aviateur
Une mauvaise manipulation et on se retrouve à vivre le sort d'un autre
    terrien, sans même savoir pourquoi
Loin de nos admirations d'origine, on se dit que l'évolution du goût, du
    cerveau est mise à l'épreuve, que c'est en lançant la balle avec force
    qu'on gagnera ce tournoi
Si l'on croit aveuglément, si l'on se jette avec défi dans le combat de la
    volonté
Notre corps aura existé seulement
Pour être guidé mécaniquement sans nécessité de croire autrement
Et pourtant, si la télécommande se brise
Quel autre mode de fonctionnement allez-vous suivre ?
Au milieu de ces débris et de notre futur désormais vide de couleurs et
    de formes
Se jeter dans le vide paraîtra comme une libération, celle de ne pas savoir
    ce qu'il en sera de la nouvelle réforme
Plus de divinité vers qui se tourner
Aucune garantie que notre mort aura été jugée bonne à un moment
    bien défini
Les muscles se disent autonomes, les sens se disent explorations, les clichés
À la con se disent bien démolis
J'ai bien compris

Que certains signes ne viennent pas pour être tempérés
Qu'ils valent la peine d'être pris en compte
Mais entre la peur de découvrir ce qui surpasse un soi-disant destin qui
    dompte
Et la décision de lâcher une partie du noyau qui obstrue nos phares
Le contraste est grand
Je ne prétends pas dire que notre force imprègnera son encre sur tous
    nos murs
Tous nos cadrans
Certains tomberont, comme certains resteront
Au final, on lance la balle, on pratique la trajectoire
Mais nul destin
Nul libre-arbitre n'arrivera forcément à nous conduire vers la bonne
    manière de fixer une balançoire

MEDEA

In the expansion of literacy, of an alphabet, of debates around the human
  nature and condition
Came one of the first forms of performance as we now know it, one
  that centers around a story, a position
The pieces of words on a text so *tragic* gave place to two to three actors
  wearing masks, symbols of imitation
Gave place to an audience fixing the stage, receiver of the catharsis, this
  succession of pitied emotions
Gave place to the voice of the *polis*, known as the chorus, beholder of
  the comments unexpressed, of the chants longed to be heard, of the
  provocative questions
Indeed, amongst the power of the gods lies a character of human form,
  with thoughts and intentions
This protagonist has been placed into the plot, neither good nor filled
  with demons
But for which his destiny, his fatality cannot be avoided, how big the
  gestures may be
Stuck in a particular structure of peripeteia, the light at the end of the
  tunnel he cannot yet see
From a bad outcome to the curse on a family tree, this misery has been
  planned out, no charity will cancel this out, only death, sadness, and
  flesh will remain
As Aristotle perceived it, success of destruction is in the simplicity of a
  plot, the genius behind the number one we gain
Never would they transport themselves from an island to a kingdom,
  never would they skip so fast the hours that exist in a day, never would
  they focus on multiple problems at a time
The three unities rule, that is the climb
But might I point out what never stood out as a concern?
The injustice in creating female characters incapable of wisdom but
  guided by tempted impulsions that burn
The injustice in their inability to play, to watch, to be a part of something
  bigger
There is a presence of contradictions, wanting to reflect a community, a
  democracy but forgetting to include their sisters, their mother
This very reflection may come back to the core of a famous theatrical
  piece, *Medea*, still staged to this day

Euripides cannot speak at this moment; we will never know for sure the
intentions behind the representation of this woman and her weight
Might it have been written as a feminist narrative, whether of conscious
or unconscious motive?
Might the author have wished to place the woman in a powerful role,
giving her the will to drive her own locomotive,
But in fearing the exterior judgments, have associated her with crimes
and witchcraft?
Maybe this version of Jason being the bad guy isn't just a simple draft
This interpretation is out in the open, and it is with the glorious mentalities
of our era that the reassurance of it being the only one comes along
But in studying this objective work with my subjective brain, I have
given up on this version for so long
In facing the destiny of both characters, of the core of their thinking
and feeling, I wished to say both have lost as much as both caused
the tragedy of it all
The male figure and the detachment he felt toward his companion when
the kids appeared on the family wall
Indeed, he abandoned and betrayed their union
The woman figure and the fear and anger she felt when her loved one
vanished, leaving her in a confused illusion
Indeed, blinded by her hurting, she destructed the fruits of a specific
lineage, the next managers
All these actions emerged in a specific context, surrounded by parameters
of an intense caliber
Jason's disrespect was at fault
Medea's impulsive deeds were at fault
Through this mechanism of human behaviors, I don't think the author
purposely wanted the first character to win more than the second
Their actions caused chaos all by themselves, I reckon
And it is crazy to think this story makes sense in the present moment
It is crazy to think statistically speaking, a lot of men leave their wives,
a lot of men prefer their children
It is crazy to think murder victims of our contemporary lives are usually
the cause of issues around the family, and through anger they are
being ridden
And if that wasn't enough, there are the stereotypes of the men of reason
and the women of passion that have not been created out of the haze

These constructed roles in society have always existed and haven't yet
    been demolished nowadays
I firmly believe Euripides was an intellectual, a philosopher, an observer
    and that his words, now shared into the world so many times didn't
    mean to be at the midpoint of a debate, over his views and
    preferences
Because in the end, Jason lost everything and so did Medea, both being
    social representatives

OXYMORONS DON'T MEAN DISTANCE

It is in your quietness and the resonance of your laughter
It is in my stubbornness and hearing the advice you were after
Your voice urgently persists to fight
Against the thunder that keeps building its way up
You let the tears translate themselves into joy, you might
Consider keeping them intact in a cup
My head strongly keeps the spine
In a straight line
Making it difficult for the receptors to take in the sides
I let others expand my horizons, I might consider perceiving them as
    guides
Taking a closer look, the angelic voice attracts the most traumatic histories
Looking from afar, the grounded posture leaks the undiscovered mysteries
From the headaches, there is no space for you to sing
From the mumbles, there is no space for me to know your take on a
    ring
Fire is your element, keeping it all bottled up is your specialty
Earth is my element, passivity is essentially part of my identity
The oxymoron lies in the possible vocal communication of two deaf
The oxymoron lies in the incapacity to cook for a chef
The table in the kitchen is not our only barrier, standing between our
    undeniable needs
The room is the only remedy for our lack of expression, wanting to get
    rid of all the deeds
Only the rhythm of our hearts can tell apart the seconds, can reassemble
    our souls
Let the sweat run through our pores and make us forget we belong to
    opposite poles

MASCULINITÉ EN DOUBLE

Deux clignotants te sont présentés quelle
Manivelle vas-tu déclencher?
Le bel
Homme que tu es, ton choix est double, ta nature déjantée
Celle qui te promet des pulsions
Mais hélas au prix d'un détour
Ou celle qui te promet des insatisfactions
Mais hélas au prix d'un trajet auquel tu peux avoir recours
Haut ou bas, la définition de ta masculinité en dépend, il te faut au volant
    une grippe bien ferme
En un instant, ta réputation peut voir le jour, sortir de sa taverne
Tu pourrais aussi bien ignorer les lumières
Te foutre à terre et risquer de t'aplatir contre la lâcheté
Défier les lois de la société, te positionner en plein milieu du danger
Moi qui pensais avoir affaire à deux cerveaux distincts
Il se peut qu'on fasse désormais de la place à un clandestin
Inconnu aux yeux de tous, loin des impulsions et du détachement par
    sélection
Sauras-tu ignorer les remarques, les uns et autres qui auront déjà accumulé
    toute une collection
Sauras-tu ignorer cette constante envie de tout posséder
De trophées de chasse, d'animaux empaillés, de conquêtes étalées
Fais abstraction de tout ce qu'on t'a enseigné
De cette perception acquise par l'héritage
Réalise les klaxonnements qui rugissent derrière toi
Tu le sais au fond de toi
La vérité derrière les virages

INTOUCHABLE, EST-CE L'ADJECTIF DE LA FEMME ?

Prisonnière de cette humidité
L'orange du bord de la fenêtre m'a tourmentée
Aucune tache de saison
Elle ne s'est pas laissé pourrir par la raison
Recouverte de son manteau d'agrume
Elle garde sa place à travers l'imperceptible brume
Indomptable, inconcevable, produit de consommation
Bien destiné à pourrir sous les rayons
Temps d'hiver, perte de la chaleureuse empathie
Son prix pris pour acquis
Dénuée de dizaines, de centaines
Sa rondeur, sa valeur attire seulement momentanément la clientèle
L'on pense aux tropiques, au jus de l'extase
Mais l'on en fait vite notre esclave
De la fenêtre, je me prends à vouloir lui tendre les mains, à les recouvrir
    d'une chair digne de l'aristocrate
Mais après avoir si vite pensé haut et fort, je me rends compte de la saleté
    qui gratte
À l'œil elle est si belle
Autant qu'elle reste ainsi à poser jusqu' à ce que le cycle fasse d'elle son
    modèle
Ses cris acérés me réveillent en pleine nuit
Ses cris m'incitent à l'observer de la vitrine qui reluit
Un trompe l'œil, une sirène me ramenant à l'époque des marins si
    facilement manipulés
Un acide qui brûle les ligaments, une tombée soudaine dans le gouffre de
    mes illusions défigurées
Le parfum des saveurs grandioses a une fin
La famine gourmande est tombée raide dingue devant le dessin
Le créateur me regarde d'en haut, aux éclats de la réussite de son coup de
    génie
De simples coups de crayons, la mine aiguisée sous la pression de berner
La peinture tentée de projeter
Les gouttes du déni
Et moi je pleure de honte, un embarras bien fort que d'avoir cru en la
    bonté de mes sens
Plus jamais je ne ferai confiance
Au renard
Au coup de deux je rejoindrai la méfiance du regard
Le touchable, la diffusion d'une rance réalité que l'on ne veut pas visionner
L'intouchable, les passages d'une trame narrative qu'on a à notre guise
    fusionné

NUANCES D'AMOUR

On peut aimer une personne loin de nous tout en espérant ne jamais la
    retrouver
On peut se languir de son étreinte comme on peut craindre d'étouffer
On peut apprécier la solitude derrière son absence pour mieux goûter
    à sa présence
On peut parler dans le vide avec le souhait qu'il n'arrive point à trouver
    la virgule
Dans cette bulle d'incohérence
On peut se mettre à vouloir jeter des yeux doux au serveur du coin
Pour faire une mise au point
On peut se laisser valser par les intonations de son rire
Tout en voulant fuir
Le tango de ses lèvres surgir
On peut laisser la haine du train de vie nous faire dépérir sans pour autant
    vouloir s'aventurer dans les bois des doigts
On peut cumuler les peines et les défauts tout en pensant qu'on n'attirerait
    point d'autres choix
On peut se réveiller la tête lourde à force de combler les attentes
Et pourtant notre peau rejoint la fontaine d'une image éclatante
On peut se rouler dans une neige glacée à percussion
Tout en suivant du doigt les braises remontant jusqu'aux poumons
On peut se mettre à tracer les spirales du plaisir
Avec délicatesse sans s'imaginer vieillir
On peut avoir craché des mots dans le creux de la main
Et se rendre compte de l'amertume du lendemain
On peut avoir trouvé passion au plus proche carré
Mais se demander ce qu'il y a au-delà des marées surnagées
On peut apprendre à connaître de fond en comble le contenu du verre
Et réaliser que l'idée du soi est bien plus sévère
On peut être tenté de se droguer au parfum de marque luxueuse
Tout en sachant que le serpent est de nature sinueuse
On peut avoir succombé à la maladie de la dépendance
N'empêche que le désir de s'éloigner se dit évidence
On peut desserrer les vis d'un pont
Tout en l'imaginant flotter au-dessus du plancton
On peut vouloir colorer les cercles du normal
Et se dire que la beauté vise plus loin que le neuronal
On peut préférer cacher les insectes qui rongent sous une pierre humide
Tout en attendant que les corps qui se mélangent les rendent lucides

On peut imaginer
se laisser bercer
par la définition du mot
Tout en repoussant d'une main brusque l'anneau
On peut se rendre aveugle aux angles aigus pourtant bien visibles
Alors qu'en réalité la foudre qui tombe nous semble fortement irrésistible

105

On peut imaginer
se laisser bercer
par la définition du mot
Tout en repoussant d'une main brusque l'anneau
On peut se rendre aveugle aux angles aigus pourtant bien visibles
Alors qu'en réalité la foudre qui tombe nous semble fortement irrésistible

PENSÉES DESTRUCTRICES

Une balade en voiture
Un coup de volant brusque en gravure
Une aventure dans les profondes maritimes
Une suspension dans le courant légitime
Une cuisine qui se perd au travers de la chaleur des vapeurs
Un effleurement ravageur
Le granite d'un mur parfaitement inégal
Le récepteur d'un coup à caractère viscéral
Des lèvres remuant les recoins de l'âme
La pression des dents que la culpabilité réclame
L'épine majestueuse du cactus
Le magnétisme du tentacule envers ce frissonnant infarctus
Les milliers de brins d'or qui forment un tout
Des instincts animaliers qui épargnent le cou
La peau qui protège le monde de l'homme
Ce sérum insoutenable qui consomme
L'ajustement des fragments de tissu
La montée des crans en continu
sur le sablier ossu
Un agrippement affectif
L'écrasant contrôle de l'addictif
Une marche inconsciente sous les luminaires
Le doux repos de la terre judiciaire
Le papier finement coupé du savoir
La gestuelle sanguinolente commise au purgatoire

NOSTALGIA STUCK IN TIME

So black and white, so adjusted according to a studied perspective
So stuck in one place, only the eye of the beholder turns fragments into
an introspective
Covered of a longing loving protection
The underworld will not be able to modify
No need to look back nor rush forward
The emotion filters have already been placed, you cannot deny
The unworried aura you once felt, the comforting pressure on your
shoulders that you thought you could never escape
Stuck in traffic, present in the now, scrape the material all you want,
some belong to die with a memory tape
Better is the spitting truth of an era than the superficial reconstruction of a
souvenir
Wrongly pushed, wrongly captured, wrongly posed, wrongly shared,
wrongly slurred
A gold object represented in an art show, the ultimate response to the
narration blurred
Editing may appease your wishes of *grandeur,*
Hide the only slur
None is forgotten in the deepness of the connections
Of the projections
All will be remembered
To the core of the spirit from the tangling nostalgia of a past well-guarded

ACKNOWLEDGEMENTS

I want to thank my family and friends who have helped me be the person I am today.

Without your support and encouragement, this project would not have seen the light of the world that exists outside of a room, of a computer, of a brain in motion.

To you my sister, all is well on this earth, and wherever you are at this moment, I hope another angel is keeping you company. Be sure that I'm always

Holding onto the density of your laugh in the air

Holding onto your sweet words echoing in my heart

ABOUT ATMOSPHERE PRESS

Atmosphere Press is an independent, full-service publisher for excellent books in all genres and for all audiences. Learn more about what we do at atmospherepress.com.

We encourage you to check out some of Atmosphere's latest releases, which are available at Amazon.com and via order from your local bookstore:

Melody in Exile, by S.T. Grant

Covenant, by Kate Carter

Near Scattered Praise Lies Our Substantial Endeavor, by Ron Penoyer

Weightless, Woven Words, by Umar Siddiqui

Journeying: Flying, Family, Foraging, by Nicholas Ranson

Lexicon of the Body, by DM Wallace

Controlling Chaos, by Michael Estabrook

Almost a Memoir, by M.C. Rydel

Throwing the Bones, by Caitlin Jackson

Like Fire and Ice, by Eli

Sway, by Tricia Johnson

A Patient Hunger, by Skip Renker

Lies of an Indispensable Nation: Poems About the American Invasions of Iraq and Afghanistan, by Lilvia Soto

The Carcass Undressed, by Linda Eguiliz

Poems That Wrote Me, by Karissa Whitson

Gnostic Triptych, by Elder Gideon

For the Moment, by Charnjit Gill

Battle Cry, by Jennifer Sara Widelitz

I woke up to words today, by Daniella Deutsch

Never Enough, by William Guest

Second Adolescence, by Joe Rolnicki

ABOUT THE AUTHOR

Allison Aube-Martin is a twenty-one-year-old storyteller who discovered her first landmarks in Paris, formulated her identity and expression in Montreal, and is now temporarily settled in New York. While growing up, this French-Canadian adored reading since it permitted her both to travel elsewhere and to understand the world that surrounded her. It wasn't long after that she began exploring her own voice and was overtaken by the need to write for others and to be read. Words, she finds, are the gates to confronting a reality that may or may not be ours, but that still exists in some form.

As she says: "I want them to relate or disconnect, but to still enjoy the journey at the end of the page."